Chateau Marmont - Mercer Hotel - Sunset Beach

Photography by Michael Mundy
Creative Direction by Jan-Willem Dikkers

Chateau Marmont

Mercer Hotel

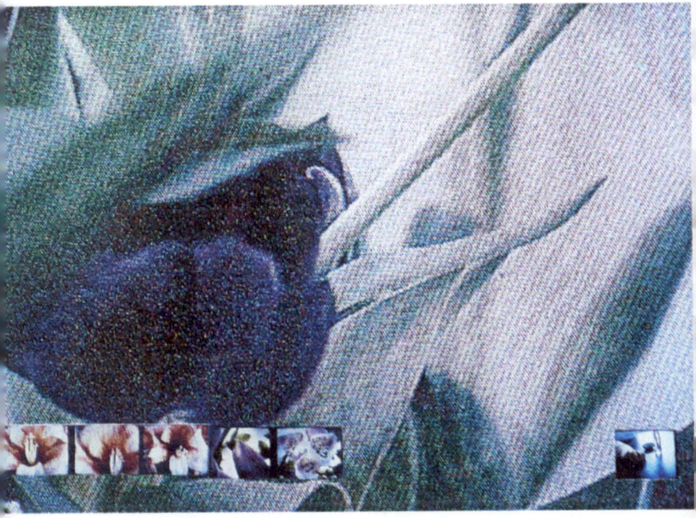

Sunset Beach

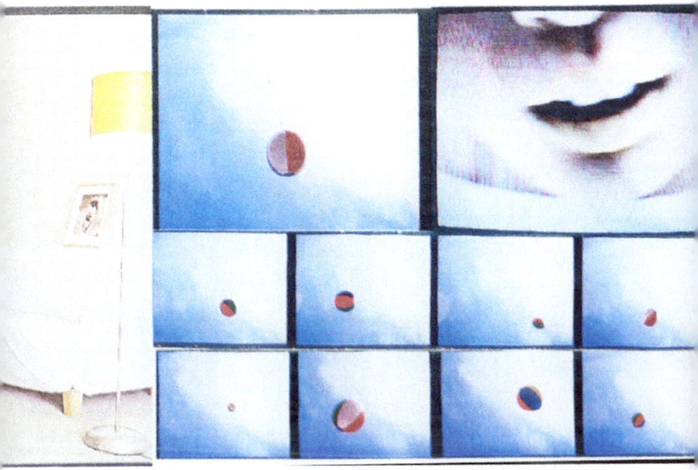

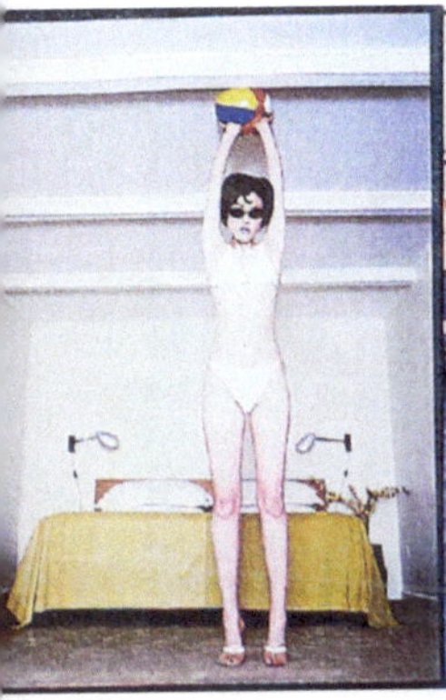

www.ingramcontent.com/pod-product-compliance
Lightning Source LLC
Chambersburg PA
CBHW042232090526
44587CB00006B/156
* 9 7 8 1 7 3 4 8 5 1 9 0 8 *